CW01654548

CHINA

from Cornwall & Devon

An illustrated account of the modern China Clay Industry

by Charles Thurlow

First Published 1992
Second (Revised) Edition 1997 – Third (Revised) Edition 2001
Fourth (Revised) Edition 2005

ISBN 1 900147 42 4

CORNISH HILLSIDE PUBLICATIONS

Typesetting & Design by The Design Field, Poggio San Marcello, Italy
www.thedesignfield.com
Printed by Short Run Press Limited, Exeter, Devon EX2 7LW

Contents **Page No.**

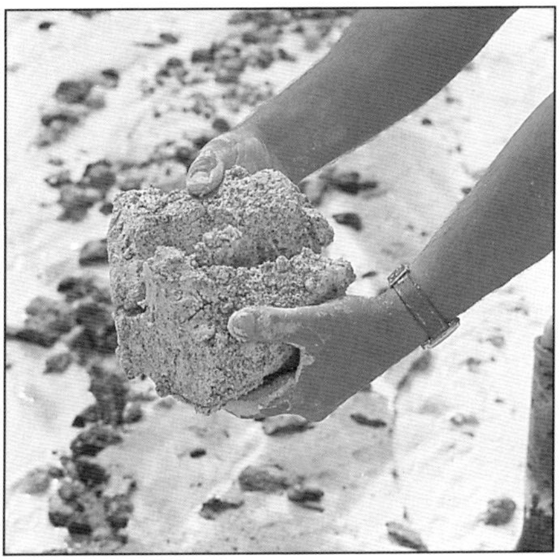

A handful of decomposed granite before washing.

Cover picture:
The front cover shows a pit face being dug out for transfer by dumper to a washing point.

PREFACE

Cornwall and Devon produce over two million tons annually of china clay, a fine white powder, for use by the paper, ceramic and many other industries. China clay is a major raw material export for the United Kingdom second only to North Sea oil and gas.

Although historical accounts have been published, the revolution in china clay technology since the 1950s had not previously been covered except for articles in technical journals. This is a revised and enlarged edition of a book first printed in 1992. The aim of the 2005 edition is, as before, to provide the layman with information about today's industry. Since 1992 many technical advances have been made and are referred to in this edition.

Acknowledgements

The author is grateful to many colleagues from the china clay industry for their advice and assistance in the preparation of this book. Photographs and illustrations are reproduced with the kind permission of Imerys Minerals and the map below courtesy of Professor C.M. Bristow and Wheal Martyn China Clay Museum.

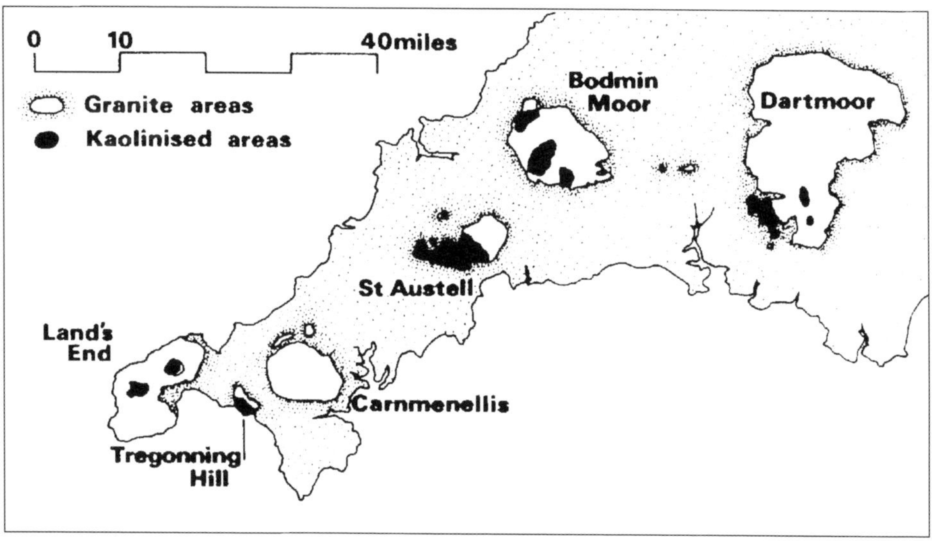

Map showing kaolinised areas of Devon & Cornwall.

BACKGROUND

Geology

The granite moors of Devon and Cornwall, when first formed about 300 million years ago, contained three main minerals, feldspar, quartz and mica. In some parts of this granite the white feldspar has since been decomposed to a soft white material. This very fine size mineral is called kaolinite and is the main constituent of china clay. The glassy, angular quartz and the platy, silver-brown micas are practically unaltered by the process of kaolinisation but very small amounts of fine particle size quartz and mica are also present in the inert, white powder called china clay. China clay is extremely fine. The particle size of china clay is measured in microns or millionths of a metre.

For two centuries geologists debated how feldspar was altered to china clay. Two theories were proposed. The hydrothermal theory was that kaolinisation took place as the result of hot chemical laden gases and fluids rising from below ground, through the granite, soon after it was formed. The other proposition was that china clay had been formed as a result of weathering from ground level at a geological time when the climate was hot and humid. After much scientific research it is now clear that a sequence of events took place which includes both theories.

The hydrothermal action came first and began the alteration process as well as introducing metalliferous deposits such as tin ores and quartz/tourmaline veins which are a distinctive feature of most china clay pits. Tourmaline is a black boron containing mineral. A stage of weathering took place afterwards when water from the surface entered cracks in the rocks. This was warmed at depth by heat due to the unusually high content of radioactive elements in the granite. A slow convective circulation of water resulted which, over hundreds of millions of years, altered feldspar to kaolin. Kaolin is a hydrated aluminium silicate and can be represented by the chemical formula $Al_2O_32SiO_22H_2O$.

History

China clay from Cornwall came into use in the mid eighteenth century when its value as a component in hard, white porcelain was recognised by a Plymouth chemist, William Cookworthy. He used it in porcelain and was later followed by many other English potters who used it in various 'recipes'. The amount of china clay produced in Devon and Cornwall gradually increased especially as additional uses were found. The rate of production rose sharply from the mid nineteenth century, when china clay began to be used by the cotton industry, and as a filler in the manufacture of paper on a large scale. It received a further boost in the twentieth century, when fine particle size clay production was pioneered, for use as a coating for smooth white paper.

Several parts of the granite moors in south-west England have kaolinised areas. All of these have been worked for china clay in the past but production is now restricted to areas around St Austell and the edge of Dartmoor.

The earliest way of clay working was to dig clay bearing ground using hand tools and take it to an area where it was worked with a diverted stream of water. Clay and sand produced a milky suspension. The coarser sand settled out and was taken away in wheelbarrows. The clay was refined in a series of settling pits and thickened in shallow tanks before drying naturally in the open air or open sided shelters called air dries. As clay pits grew Cornish beam engines were used to pump a clay suspension from pits and inclined railways carried sand away to tips. Long buildings with floors heated by coal fires were built to dry the clay more quickly. Some of these methods can be seen in the China Clay Museum at Wheal Martyn near St. Austell.

Numerous companies were involved, working over one hundred small pits and the development of improved methods was slow. During the last eighty years the number of companies involved in the industry declined, as mergers and take-overs took place. Today all production comes from one large and two smaller companies who operate about twenty pits, many formed by the merging of small pits. In the second half of the twentieth century, the need for increased tonnages of high quality clay and reduced labour costs led to the introduction of more complex and advanced methods of working china clay. The industry now has the capacity to produce two and a half million tons of china clay per year and the techniques in general use today, are the subject of this publication.

The processing of china clay can be divided into three main phases. Clay pits 'wash' decomposed granite to produce raw clay which is fed to central refining units. Here clay is improved to meet customers' requirements using a range of processes. After refining it is piped to large drying plants where it is dried and stored to await distribution or extra treatment.

Prospecting

In former times the existence of clay and its quality in the granite moorlands of Cornwall and Dartmoor, was checked by digging small pits and trenches. This could only give a superficial indication of the amount of clay present.

Today a preliminary assessment can be made by geophysical prospecting, a technique where the electrical resistivity of the ground is measured. Kaolinised granite is a good conductor of electricity, but unkaolinised granite is a poor conductor. A survey of this kind indicates where china clay may be found and is also valuable in showing areas of hard rock where tips and buildings might be located. Following this, the clay-bearing ground is tested using drills capable of cutting out cores of rock which can be brought up to the surface. These cores are tested to check the quality of the clay and variations with depth. Depths up to 240 metres have been tested in this way. The results of drilling can be used to calculate the reserves of clay available in a given area.

Cores drilled from china clay bearing ground being examined and placed in boxes to await testing.

1. PIT OPERATIONS

Summary

In a china clay pit kaolinised granite is broken up by water jets which result in a mixture of clay and sand in suspension running to a low point in the pit. The clay and sand are then separated in the pit area. The clay fraction is pumped away for further refining and the sand is taken to tips.

Part of a large clay pit with streams of clay, water and sand flowing towards sand removal plant. The side of the pit is benched for safe working.

Removing Overburden

Decomposed granite of workable quality, is usually overlain by a brown stained layer of the same material which is capped by a layer of topsoil. These layers called overburden, have to be removed before the extraction of white china clay can take place. The topsoil is stockpiled for use in landscaping work on sites where clay extraction has been completed.

A shovel loader with a 9 cubic metre bucket is filling dumpers with up to 65 tonnes of overburden. Even larger loaders and dumpers are now coming into use.

Breaking up Hard Ground before Washing

The decomposed granite found in clay pits is by no means uniform. It contains veins of minerals such as quartz and tourmaline and islands of largely unaltered granite. All this material has to be moved, to allow a pit to develop safely.

Most ground is broken up by drilling holes of 150mm diameter with a machine which uses a hard tungsten carbide tipped drill and jointed drilling steels to enable holes with depths up to 15m to be drilled.

Drilling a series of holes for blasting. The rig comprises a compressor and drill mounted on a mast which also holds drill steels.

The small piles of fine sand and dust produced during drilling can be used to check the quality of clay. For blasting, holes are charged with explosive emulsion produced on site in truck mixers.

Dry Mining

In recent years some larger pits have adpoted a system known as dry mining where kaolinised granite is dug by an excavator usually after blasting. The granite is taken to a fixed 'make down' site where washing takes place and is followed by removal of stones and sand.

A large excavator with a 6.5 cu. m. bucket loading 50 tonne six wheel, all wheel drive dumpers for transfer to a make down plant.

A smaller excavator with 3 cu. m. bucket loading, 25 tonne dumpers.

Make Down Plants

Make down plants range from traditional washing by a monitor of material stockpiled by dumpers to purpose built facilities, depending on local requirements. In the latter, dumpers with kaolinised granite from dry mining tip into a hopper. Here a number of small water jets break down the granite releasing clay, sand and stones. The stones are separated by vibrating screens or rotating trommels. Sands are separated by bucket wheel classifiers described later.

Large Make Down plant.

Washing the Clay Face – The Traditional Method

Some pits use an older process to direct a jet of water onto the clay face. A 'monitor' controlled by an operator in a cabin uses a water pressure up to 300psi (20 bar) is provided by large centrifugal pumps which use recycled water.

A monitor washing clay with a shovel loader stockpiling stent to one side. Operator's cabin is on the left hand side.

As washing proceeds hard, unaltered rock known as 'stent' accumulates at the foot of the washing face. This rock together with rock from large veins and islands, already mentioned, is taken out of the pit using shovel loaders and dumpers.

Ripping

A bulldozer pushing ground. Ripper tooth can be seen to the rear.

Another method of breaking softer ground is to use a bulldozer equipped with a steel claw at the back, known as a ripper. The bulldozer alternately uses the ripper to break up the ground and then the front blade to push the broken ground towards the point where washing takes place.

Uses for Rock

Some large rocks can find use as 'armour' stone when they are placed to minimise the effects of wave action in coastal defence schemes.

About 1.6 million tonnes of rock are sold annually after crushing and grading. About 70% of aggregates used in Cornwall for road construction are derived from china clay pits.

Rocks which have been selected for size and hardness stockpiled as armour stone.

A shovel loader on the left places rock into a jawcrusher. The product is screened into various grades.

Gravel Pumping

The wash of china clay, sand and mica in suspension, flows to the lowest point in the pit where it is pumped to a higher level by centrifugal pumps. These consist of a circular impeller inside a circular casing. Wash is drawn from a shallow pond of accumulated material, through a suction pipe, to the centre of the gravel pump. The impeller pushes it through a delivery pipe, which is moulded to the edge of the casing.

A gravel pump with 250mm inlet and outlet pipes. The design of the impeller allows stones of up to 150mm to be pumped.

Gravel pump mounted on tracks pumping from the bottom of a pit to a sand removal system.

Gravel pumps deliver wash to a sand removal plant, often located in the bottom of pits. In some cases, a series of gravel pumps is used to lift the wash to the top of the pit away from clay bearing ground, for the sand removal stage.

Sand Removal - General

Older methods of sand removal involved settling sand from clay in special troughs or pits and after settling, removing the sand in small wagons. These were pulled out of the pit on inclined railways and tipped nearby. This was a slow and laborious process that was gradually replaced from the late 1950's. Many clay works today use bucket wheel classifiers that remove sand from the wash continuously and work in conjunction with conveyor belts. Other works use large settling pits where the sand is removed by shovel loaders and dumpers. Conveyors and dumpers allow the sand to be carried away from clay bearing ground for sale to the building industry or onto tips.

Bucket Wheel Classifiers

The bucket wheel classifier works on the principle that in water containing a mixture of sand, mica and clay the coarsest particles, which are quartz, sand and undecomposed feldspar, will settle more quickly than the finer particles of clay and mica.

Bucket wheel in centre, clay overflow on right, sand dewatering screen and a conveyor on left.

Above: A bucket wheel installation showing dewatering screens and a conveyor belt.

Left: A bucket wheel picking up sand from the trough. Clay and water drains through the slotted sides of the buckets.

The bucket wheel desander with a wheel six metres in diameter moves slowly and picks up sand from the bottom of a trough in buckets attached to the perimeter of the wheel. Again finer particles overflow the trough and go to the next stage of treatment.

Sand removed is placed on vibrating screens, which drain further water from the sand.

After screening the sand drops onto a system of conveyor belts, which either take it to tips, to a sand grading plant, or to a stockpile where it is loaded into dumpers for tipping. The conveyor belts are made of rubber reinforced with synthetic fibres.

The final section of a conveyor system is a 'spreader' mounted on caterpillar tracks which can tip sand over a wide area.

Sand Pits

An alternative to classifiers and conveyors is the use of sand pits where sand is allowed to settle in an enclosed area which is formed by walls of sand and rock and is located not far from the lowest part of the pit. The wash is pumped into these pits by gravel pumps. Here the clay and mica overflow the pits via a vertical wooden launder (pipe). The sand settles in the pit and weir boards are used to gradually raise the height of the launder. A thick bed of sand builds up which, after a period of drainage, is loaded by shovel loaders into dumpers and taken to a sand tip. Works using this system will have two or more adjoining pits of this type so that one can be filling whilst another is draining or being emptied. This method uses mobile plant occasionally rather than a continuous system of classifiers and conveyors.

Sand pits in operation. The right hand pit with a launder on the extreme right is filling whilst the left hand pit is being emptied.

Proportions of Clay, Rock and Sands

The working of china clay results in large quantities of rock, sand and mica being produced as well. Whenever possible, uses are sought for such materials. Some of these by-products have to be put onto tips or used for backfilling disused pits. The ratio of china clay to by-products varies from pit to pit depending largely on the degree of kaolinisation encountered. It is generally as follows, giving a ratio of about 1:9

China clay 1
Rock 4.5
Sand 3.5
Mica 1

The product called mica is a mixture of fine sand, mica flakes and some coarse kaolin. The separation and storage of mica is discussed later.

Uses for Sand

Just over 500,000 tonnes of sand, from china clay workings are sold annually and is widely used in Cornwall and Devon. There would be scope for greatly increased sales of this sand if the cost of transport to more distant markets could be reduced.

Sand works producing graded sands. Pit sand is brought to this washing plant by conveyor in the right foreground.

The sand is widely used by the building industry and there are eight sand plants working in the china clay areas of Cornwall and Devon. These provide products such as gravels and grits as well as medium and fine sands to British Standard Specifications.

Sand plants use vibrating screens for coarser products and hydrocyclone classifiers, to be described shortly, for finer sands.

Sand customers include ready-mixed concrete makers and the manufacturers of concrete products such as paving slabs and kerbs. Total sales of sand include 200,000 tonnes of sand from china clay workings used annually in the manufacture of concrete blocks.

Plants for coated road aggregates (foreground) and concrete block manufacture (background).

A tip site where topsoil has been taken off and herring bone pattern drains constructed.

Tipping of Rock and Sands

Before tipping begins the ground to be used is checked by trenching and drilling. This is necessary to establish what drainage is required so that water will not build up within the tip. After the removal of topsoil most tips have a herringbone pattern of drains cut into the ground which are filled with crushed stone. Other considerations such as height, slope and volume are planned in advance of tipping.

Tips are built in layers each around 25 metres in height. Upper layers are placed inside lower layers so that the final slope after profiling is much less than the natural angle of repose of the material in the tip.

Pumping Clay through Pipelines

Clay is pumped over considerable distances within the Devon and Cornwall clay producing areas. Centrifugal pumps send clay through steel or plastic pipelines, varying from 200mm to 450mm in diameter, so that clay can be pumped from pits to refiners and from refiners to drying plants. Over 200 miles of pipeline are currently in use.

Stainless steel pipelines carrying clay to a refining plant.

Separation of Fine Sand and Coarse Mica

The next stage in the process is to remove fine sand and some mica from the desanded wash. To do this, the wash is pumped continuously into a

Left: A hydrocyclone which is one of 20 or more units working together to handle all the wash from a large pit.

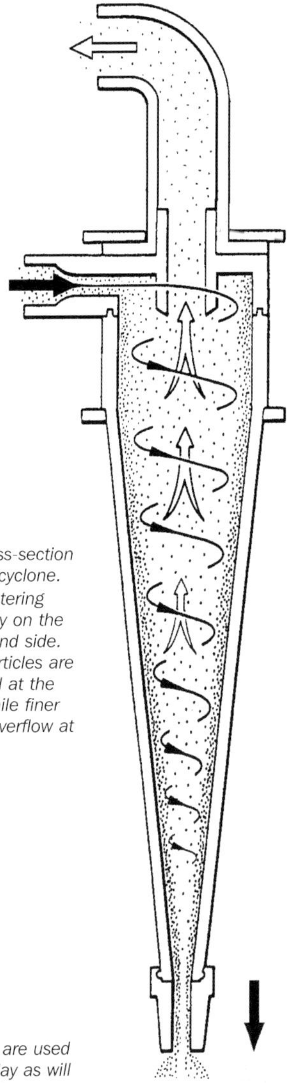

Right: Cross-section of a hydrocyclone. Feed is entering tangentially on the top left hand side. Coarse particles are discharged at the bottom while finer particles overflow at the top.

Other size hydrocyclones are used in the refining of china clay as will be seen. Generally, smaller diameter hydrocyclones are used to make finer separations.

circular, tapered pipe with a maximum internal diameter commonly of 350mm, known as a hydrocyclone or hydroclone.

The wash enters the upper part of the pipe on one side and swirls around the interior. Centrifugal forces cause the coarser particles to form a layer on the inside of the hydrocyclone casing and the swirling effect carries these particles to the tapered bottom section of the pipe, where they emerge as an umbrella shaped discharge. The finer particles of clay and mica, less affected by centrifugal forces, are displaced towards the centre of the cone and overflow through a pipe at the top.

The aim in this separation is to divide the feed into particles coarser than 50 microns (0.05 millimetres) and particles finer than 50 microns. At this size there is an almost complete separation between china clay and other minerals, such as mica and fine quartz sand, found in local kaolinised granite. The finer particles are china clay although some further sorting is needed to produce the grades of clay required by different industries. These are pumped to refining plants. The coarse underflow is pumped to mica lagoons.

Mica Lagoons

In the early days of the industry, all 'mica' from refining processes was discharged into local rivers along with some coarse sand. These effluents helped to form some large beaches in St. Austell Bay. Today all mica discharges are contained within the china clay area.

Lagoon with walls of rock and sand built round a worked out pit.

Mica from hydrocyclones and subsequent refining stages, is suspended in water and could cause instability if placed on sand tips. To contain this material, lagoons are formed, with walls built of sand and rock. Sometimes lagoon walls are built around the edge of worked out pits. The mica settles leaving a layer of clear water on the surface. This water is pumped away for reuse. The flat surfaces of lagoons can be restored to agriculture by seeding and careful management.

As new refining methods are developed, early mica lagoons are often re-worked to recover clay which was lost in the less efficient, older processes. This follows the pattern of many mining operations where old waste dumps are reworked as technological improvements take place.

Sheep grazing on a former mica lagoon after restoration.

2. REFINING PROCESSES

Summary

China clay pumped to refiners contains some finer sand and micaceous material. Refining processes are used to separate out these unwanted components. At the same time clay is sorted into grades of different quality and other processes are used to produce clays with the particle size range, flow properties, whiteness and other attributes needed by the many industries that use china clay.

A control room at a refining plant where instruments used to monitor and control processing are grouped together.

Tanks for Thickening and Refining

Circular tanks with diameters varying from 11 to 43 metres in diameter are used for thickening clay before and after refining as well as the refining process. All these tanks have a floor which slopes towards a central discharge point. The tanks are equipped with two radial, raking arms, with

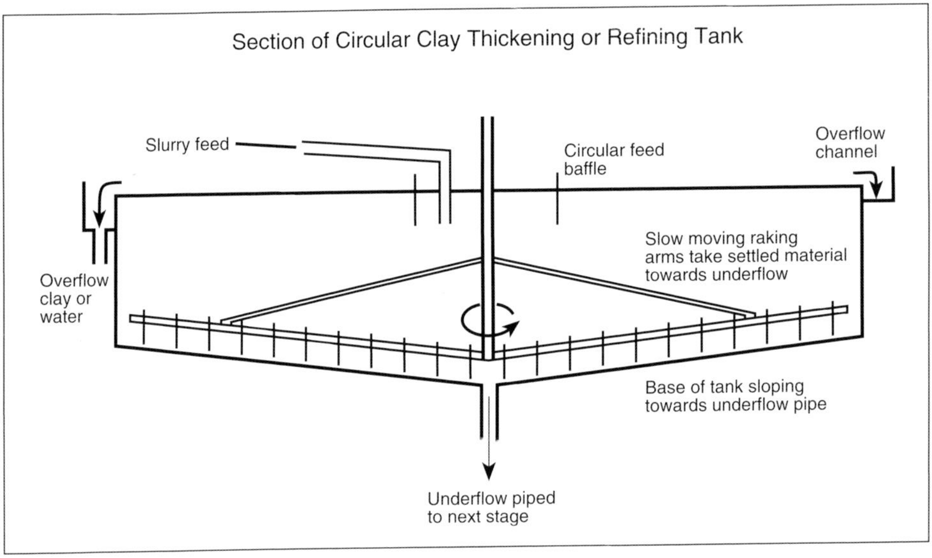

angled blades that revolve slowly and push settled material to a central outlet in the bottom of the tank.

Thickening before Refining

The clay and fine mica which overflow the hydrocyclones, is pumped continuously into the middle of large circular tanks, 43 metres in diameter These tanks are used to remove some water before the clay suspension is refined. To assist settling, a flocculant is often added to the clay in the tank. This is a chemical which encourages particles of clay to cluster together, so that they behave as larger particles and settle faster than individual particles would. At the top edge of the tank, clear water overflows into a channel which leads to a reservoir. This reservoir, called a hosepool, is the main source of water for the pumps that provide high pressure water for washing in the pit. Additional water comes from later stages of the refining and drying processes and from disused clay pits which are used to hold reserves of water. These reserves are especially important in dry summers.

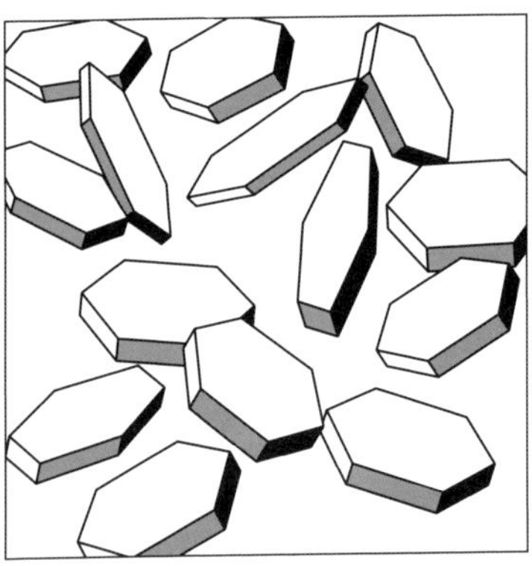

Flocculated Clay.

Such thickeners are located close to individual pits. Clay from them is pumped to one of several refining plants and is tested for various properties such as colour, particle size and viscosity. Clays from those tanks can then be blended at the refining stage with a view to producing refined clay of a particular grade.

A group of 43m diameter thickeners with an enclosed area between serving as a reservoir for overflow water.

Refining to Remove Fine Mica using Tanks (Hydroclassifiers)

In this process, a series of raked tanks are used in a continuous process of refining. These tanks are of smaller diameters, such as 15 or 21 metres. Instead of flocculating the clay fed to these tanks, the opposite process of deflocculation is employed. In this case, the particles in suspension are encouraged to repel each other, by the addition of a deflocculant, usually an alkaline chemical. The effect is that clay particles remain in suspension for some time and overflow the edge of the refining tanks. The fine mica is coarser than the clays and settles to the bottom of the tanks, where it is removed by pumps.

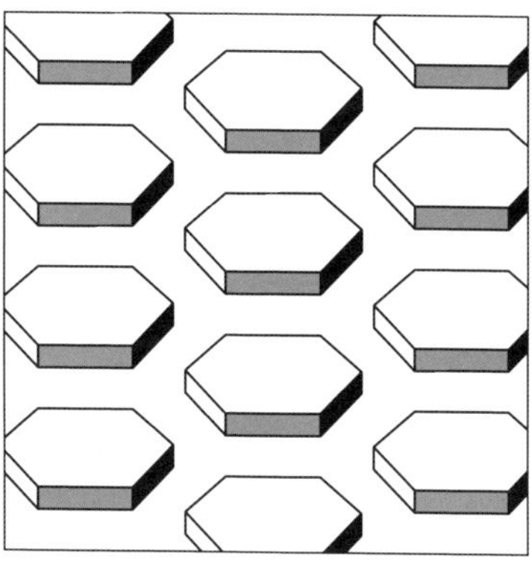

Deflocculated Clay.

To control refining and blending operations, instruments are employed. Flow rates are monitored by 'magnetic' flow meters and solids contents are measured by 'nucleonic' density gauges. Most chemical addition is assessed by 'pH' checking. All these variables are monitored and controlled from a central control room.

Some coarse clay is trapped with the

Clay overflowing the rims of refining tanks.

A group of 125mm hydrocyclones.

fine mica, so that the underflow from the refining tanks is retreated in similar tanks, to ensure that as much clay as possible is recovered. The final underflow from this process is given further treatment.

Refining to Remove Fine Mica using Hydrocyclones

An alternative method of refining thickened clay is to use hydrocyclones. These are similar to those described previously for separating fine sand but are of smaller diameter. To cope with a reasonable tonnage the clay to be treated is split up to feed a number of hydrocyclones. Initially, flocculated clay is fed to hydrocyclones with an internal diameter of 125 mm. The overflow from these is retreated in a smaller set of hydrocyclones with a 50 mm internal diameter. The underflows from both sets either go to a mica lagoon or are retreated in a sand grinding process described below.

After refining, clay is piped to further raked tanks for storage. From here the clay will be pumped to a drying plant, if it meets the specification for a particular grade of clay. Sometimes clays from different sources are blended after refining, to match a specification. Alternatively the clay may be processed further, to produce grades of clay with particular properties.

Grinding China Clay Residues

The final underflows from refining by hydroseparators or cyclones contain some large particles of china clay made up of curled stacks of finer particles. Their size is similar to the unwanted mica and sand. The clay can be recovered separately if the mixture of mica, sand and china clay is treated by a special grinding process described overleaf.

The grinding process can take advantage of the fact that the stacks of china clay particles grind much more easily than the other components. By grinding for a relatively short time the coarse kaolin only is broken down. The ground product is classified in small hydrocyclones to give a china clay overflow. The underflow is pumped to mica lagoons.

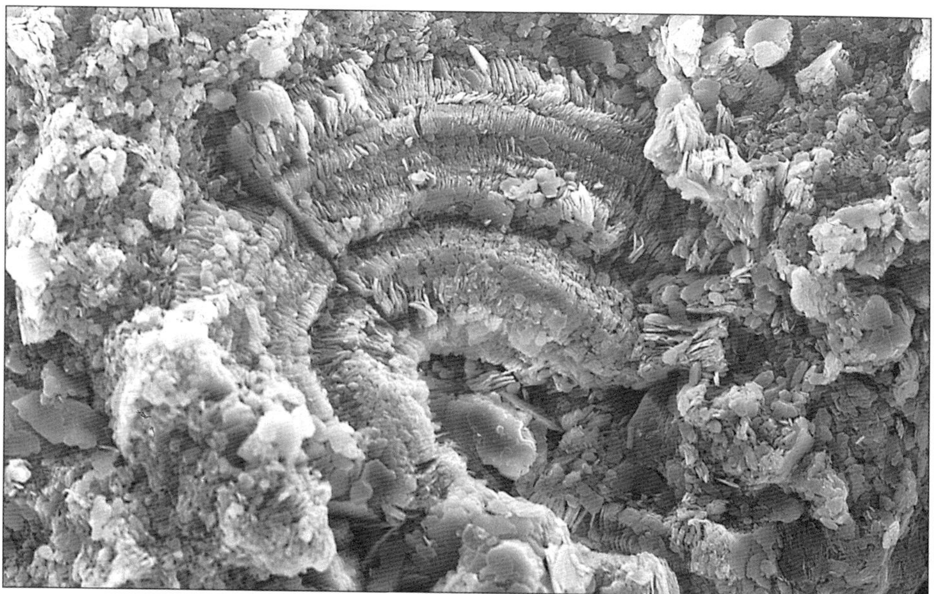

Electron microscope photograph of china clay before processing. The curled stacks of large particle clay can be recovered by grinding which delaminates the stacks. The large curled stack is 70 microns wide.

A group of sand grinding machines. Note agitator drive at the top of the machine and ground clay overflowing through screens at the top of the vessels.

Cut-away diagram of a sand grinding machine.

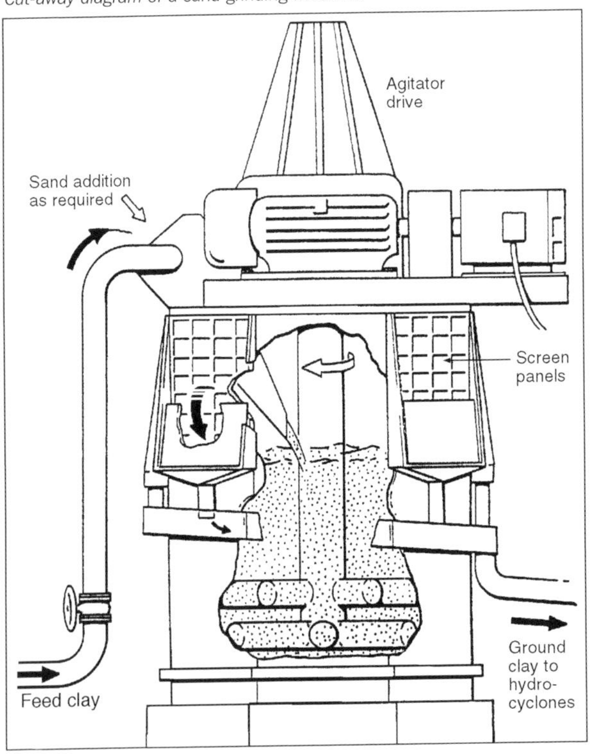

Grinding China Clay

The grinding process is also applied to refined clays where the need is to produce clays of particular fineness or 'aspect ratio'. This is the relationship between the length and thickness of clay particles. It affects the amount of clay needed to coat paper.

By careful control of the grinding machines china clays can be 'tailored' to give products with size specifications to suit different clay using industries.

In the grinding process clay residue or clays are stirred in hexagonal vessels which contain special ceramic beads These are coarser than the clay and when stirred by a rotating agitator in the vessel, break down the clay particles. These devices are known as sand grinding machines.

Clay is fed into the centre of the machine and after grinding flows out through screens around the upper part. This overflow is treated in hydrocyclones, so that any sand which overflows with the clay, can be separated.

Magnetic Separation to Improve Coarse Clays

Refined china clay can include small amounts of minerals such as mica, iron oxides and tourmaline, which all contain some iron. Such minerals can cause specks in ceramic ware when it is fired and will reduce the brightness of clay used for paper making. A powerful electromagnet can remove these iron-bearing minerals from china clay.

Two types of machine are employed. Both machines can use a super-conducting electromagnet to give a high magnetic field with a low electric current This is achieved by having an electromagnet working in very low temperature conditions such as - 267°c. Older machines are being converted to this system.

The machine employed on coarser clays, is a large electromagnet with a circular chamber in the centre, which is 2 metres wide and 500mm deep. This is filled with stainless steel wool. When clay passes through the machine, the slightly magnetic particles are attracted to the magnetised stainless steel wool and held. The electromagnet works on a cycle, with a flushing stage, where the magnet is switched off and clear water is introduced to wash away the slightly magnetic particles, through a separate discharge pipe.

A powerful magnetic separator with a static chamber. Clay rises up into the magnetised chamber and comes out through the pipes in the centre.

Magnetic Separation to Improve Fine Clays

To improve fine clays a machine with a pair of reciprocating canisters is used.

A super conducting magnetic chamber with one canister in the magnetic field and one outside.

The canisters are packed with wire wool. They are moved in and out of a super conducting magnetic field. Clay is pumped through the canister in the magnetic field and the slightly magnetic particles are held on the wire wool matrix. After about a minute this canister moves out of the magnetic field and the paired canister moves into the field. The canister outside of the field is flushed to remove magnetics before moving back into the magnetic field. This method allows clay to be treated almost continuosly.

Fine Clays for Coating Paper

China clay which is to be used for coating paper must be of particularly fine size. To achieve this, refined clay is separated into coarse and fine fractions. The fine fraction will consist largely of particles finer than two microns (two millionths of a metre) in size.

The machine used for this purpose is a centrifugal classifier usually called a centrifuge. Several types are used and one is shown in diagrammatic form below. This consists of a part circular, part tapered bowl, which is rotated at high speed. Refined clay is pumped to the centre of this bowl and the coarser particles move to the edge of the bowl, because they are more affected by centrifugal forces. Inside the bowl is a spiral screw, which is rotating at a slightly higher speed than the bowl. The screw

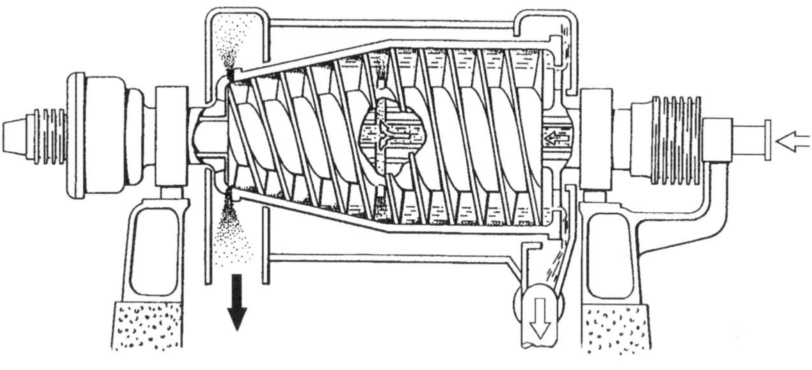

Cross section of a centrifuge. Feed clay enters on the right hand side. Coarse clay is discharged to the left, fine clay to the right.

pushes the coarser clay towards the tapered end of the bowl, where it is discharged. Fine clay overflows at the opposite end of the bowl.

These machines employ principles of gravity settling similar to those of the hydrocyclone and sand classifier, but the high speed of rotation, generates greater gravitational forces and makes a finer separation possible.

Nowadays coating clays with a range of size specifications are produced and nozzle centrifuges are used for many clays. These work on the same principle but discharge the coarser clays through small nozzles in the bowl of the centrifuge. The bowl speed of these machines is easily varied so that these machines can produce a range of products.

A nozzle centrifuge. Feed enters on the left hand side.

A vertical nozzle centrifuge.

In some plants coarse and fine centrifuge products are retreated in other centrifuges to maximise recovery of fine clay or to make clay with particular specifications. Centrifuges can also be used to thicken clay before bleaching.

Continuous Particle Size Measurement

To monitor the particle size of centrifuge products an on-line system of measurement is used. A sample is automatically collected and fed into a small conical vessel. The rate of settlement of particles is proportional to their particle size. By measuring the solids content of clay in the top of the cone using a nucleonic density gauge, the percentage of clay finer than 2 microns can be measured.

Operator checking the printed out results from on-line size measurement equipment.

Whiteness Measurement

The whiteness of a china clay sample is measured by comparing the brightness of it against a standard of known high brightness such as magnesium oxide powder. Clay brightness is sometimes reduced by staining from peat or by iron oxide compounds both of which can occur in china clay pits.

Ozone Treatment

To improve the brightness where organic staining is caused by vegetation including peat, china clay can be treated with ozone gas in a very dilute concentration.

The gas, produced on site in an ozoniser, is allowed to rise inside a tower. the ozone reacts with the discoloured organic material and oxidises it to a white colour. Any ozone which reaches the top of the tower is detected and burnt off automatically.

Ozone bleaching towers. These contain many small steel baffles to slow down the passage of clay and maximise bleaching.

Bleaching

Staining by iron oxides is more common and a bleaching process using sodium hydrosulphite converts the insoluble iron oxide into iron sulphate. This is less strongly coloured and soluble so that the iron is lost later on in the process when the clay is dewatered.

Instruments to control and record sodium hydrosulphite bleaching process.

Clay to be bleached is passed through a tower similar to that used for ozone treatment. This helps to remove air trapped in the clay and improves the efficiency of bleaching. The clay then passes through pipework where sodium hydrosulphite is added, using sophisticated instrumentation which monitors brightness for optimum dosage of this expensive chemical. This process is similar to that used by papermakers to bleach wood pulp.

Treatment of Coarse Clays by Flotation

Small amounts of abrasive minerals such as quartz could cause wear problems on the plastic mesh used by papermakers to form paper from a mixture of china clay and wood pulp. Some coarser clays are treated to remove potentially abrasive minerals.

The process used, known as flotation, is based on the addition of small amounts of chemicals to the coarse clay, which will waterproof the kaolin particles but not affect other minerals. When air bubbles are passed through such a mixture the waterproofed kaolin particles attach themselves to the air bubbles.

The process is carried out in a series of open boxes, called cells, each of which is equipped with a stirrer which helps create a flow of air bubbles within the cell. These bubbles collect waterproofed kaolin particles that rise to the top of the cell as a froth. Typically a series of six cells is used to treat coarse clay and maximise the recovery of kaolin. The particles which do not float are discarded as mica from the bottom of the end cell.

Flotation cells with recovered clay froth overflowing. The froth is broken down by water sprays.

3. DRYING PLANTS

Summary

Refined china clay is piped to drying plants where it is thickened in settling tanks. This is followed by further thickening in a filter press which produces a solid cake of china clay. The cakes are cut up and fed into a mechanical dryer. The dried clay goes to stores called linhays.

Thickening before Drying

In the refining process, some clay remains in a deflocculated state. Afterwards all clay is flocculated by using small amounts of acid, so that the clay settles quickly. This enables the clay to be thickened before the drying process begins, by removing clear water from the top of the storage tanks located at the refiners and drying units.

Dryers at Par Harbour showing from left settling tanks, Buell dryers and linhays. On the right hand side is a plant for slurry clay mentioned later. In the background, out of picture is a fluid bed dryer.

Filter Pressing to Reduce Water Content

After clay is thickened in tanks, a further stage of water reduction is used before the clay is dried. This process, known as filter pressing, is carried out by pumping the clay under pressure, into a series of chambers lined with a tightly woven nylon cloth, which will allow water, but not clay particles, to pass through. The chambers are formed by recessed plates, which may be square or circular in shape. A line of plates placed together in a framework make up a filter press.

Square & Circular Plate Presses

Filter presses with square plates have been used for the partial dewatering of china clay for many years. The plates were made of cast iron, but today plastic polypropylene plates are used. Other modern presses use circular steel plates, one metre in diameter. These plates slide on side beams. Either type uses around 120 plates per press.

Both methods of pressing have a similar system of operations. Initially the plates, 'dressed' with filter cloths, are pushed tightly together by a

Filter presses with square polypropylene plates.

hydraulic ram. Clay is then pumped through a hole in the centre of the plates and clay builds up in the chambers. As pumping pressure is maintained water in the clay suspension is encouraged to escape through the nylon filter cloths where it can trickle out through small passages in the press plate. Thickened clay builds up in the chambers and eventually forms a solid 'cake', the consistency of fresh window putty with a 25 - 30% water content. The circular plate presses produce cakes with the lower moisture level as the circular shape allows clay feed pressures of up to 1,000 psi or 68 bar. to be used in contrast to a maximum of 220 psi. or 15 bar. for square plastic plates. In both presses when a solid cake has built up, after 1 or 2 hours, the clay feed is stopped and the hydraulic ram is retracted so that the plates can be separated. The plates are moved one at a time so that the cakes of clay can be freed. Cakes tend to stick to the cloths, but are easily shifted by hand or by a small pulse of compressed air behind the cloth in circular plate presses.

A cake of clay being discharged from a circular plate press.

Filter presses are sited above a slow moving 'slat table' conveyor which take cakes to rotating knives where the cakes are cut into small slices and are transported by conveyor belts to subsequent processing stages.

Filter Pressing in a Tube Press

An alternative method of filter pressing for coarser clays, is the tube press. This consists of two tubes one inside the other, with an internal space between them, except at the bottom where the inner tube is bell shaped to fit closely within the outer tube. The inner tube contains drainage holes and is covered with a filter cloth. The outer tube has a tubular rubber bladder inside it. Clay is pumped into the space between the filter cloth and the rubber bladder. Hydraulic fluid is then pumped into the space between the outer tube and the rubber bladder. This compresses the clay and forces water through the filter cloth. The advantage of this method, is that very high pressures of up to 100 bar, can be used and the filter cake can be reduced to 18% water content. When the pressing cycle is complete, the inner tube can be lowered slightly within the outer tube and the clay cake is pushed off by compressed air.

The product is firm, easily handled and sold in this form.

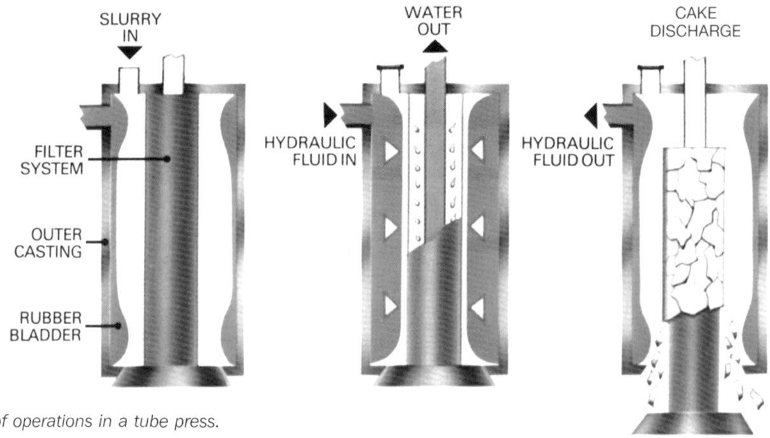

Cycle of operations in a tube press.

Banks of tube presses in the background with filtered clay on conveyors.

Treatment before drying

Clays which are to be used for paper coating are often passed through a pug mill before drying. The mill is a cylinder with a spiral rotating inside it. Clay is fed in at one end and forced towards a tapered outlet at the opposite end, where it emerges. The machine is similar in principle to a traditional kitchen mincer. The 'mincing' action tends to round particles of clay slightly and improve their flow properties. This is especially important in a coating clay, where a thin layer of clay in suspension has to flow readily onto a continuous sheet of paper moving at high speed.

A pug mill in operation. Clay enters the left hand side of the cylindrical mill in the centre and discharges onto a conveyor belt.

Final Preparation before Drying

China clay is converted to a pelletised form before drying takes place. The first stage is mixing in an enclosed trough with paddles that mix the clay and break down any lumps. Sometimes a small amount of dry 'feedback' clay is added at this stage.

A paddle mixer with four rotating shafts and paddles.

Part of a pelletiser with cover removed to show pegs.

After this stage, clay is conveyed to a drum enclosing a rotating, vertical shaft carrying pegs known as a pelletiser. These form the clay into pellets, about the size of a finger nail. This is a convenient form for drying.

Combined Heat and Power for Drying

In recent years newer dryers have been adapted to use exhaust heat from modified gas turbine engines. These engines use natural gas to provide heat and power for a number of drying units.

A combined heat and power plant with gas turbines in the lower left hand side and ducting carrying hot exhaust gases to two drying plants.

The engines are located close to dryers and are enclosed in buildings which provide sound insulation. The exhaust heat is ducted in large insulated pipes to dryers.

Most china clay dryers retain a combustion chamber for oil or gas but the combined heat and power system offers a lower cost fuel option and reduces the emissions of green house and acid rain gases compared with other fuel systems.

Buell Tray Dryer

This type of dryer was introduced in the second half of the twentieth century. The dryer consists of a stack of trays in a circular tower, rotated in a current of hot air, drawn into the dryer by fans. There are thirty layers of trays and each of these circular layers consists of a number of radial trays with gaps between them. Clay is fed into the top of the dryer. As the trays complete one revolution, the clay on them is pushed off by fixed arms onto the next layer of trays, so that the clay gradually moves down through the dryer.

Heat for drying is carried by large insulated pipes to the sides of the dryer. A flow of air is maintained by a fan, which draws air from the top of the dryer. This air passes through a special cleaning chamber, where any clay dust present is settled by fine water sprays, before the air passes out through a tall chimney.

A Buell tray drier with combustion chamber in the right foreground. A series of inspection doors allow operators to check the trays as can be seen top centre of this photograph.

After 45 minutes clay that has been through the dryer emerges from the bottom with a 10% moisture content and is carried away by a conveyor belt to a linhay.

Fluid Bed Drying with Separate Cooling

Recently introduced into the industry is a dryer in which the hot air for drying in a horizontal cylindrical chamber is introduced under slight pressure through a perforated floor. This has the effect of fluidising pellets of clay fed onto the floor. As a result the hot air is able to dry the pellets quickly and uniformly. The drying cylinder is arranged so that the perforated floor is vibrated in an elliptical motion and the bed of clay is gradually moved across the floor.

Above: On the right is a combustion chamber burning natural gas providing hot air for the fluidised bed. To the right of the drying chamber in the centre, pellets of clay are introduced. These are fluidised and gradually dry as they are vibrated to the left hand side where they discharge into a cooling chamber. Note operator looking into an inspection door.

Right: A view through the inspection door of the fluid bed dryer showing pellets entering from the right and being fluidised on the dryer floor.

The hot dried clay is transferred to another, separate fluidised chamber which uses atmospheric air to cool the clay. Tonnages of 6,000 tons per week can be dried with this dryer.

Fluid Bed Drying with Combined Cooling

Another type of fluid bed dryer uses a single fluidised bed for drying and cooling. This compact unit is best suited to lower tonnage drying e.g 3,000 tons per week.

The use of integrated drying and cooling chambers in fluid bed dryers reduces dust levels outside by minimising steam emission from dried product as it enters storage linhays.

The dryer is fed with pelletised clay on the left. The clay is dried and then cooled on the right hand side. The fan drawing cooling air is on the right of the photograph.

4. PREPARATION FOR THE CUSTOMER

Summary

China clay is sold to a wide range of industries who use it for differing purposes. Many years ago it was sold as dried, in bulk, or in barrels. Nowadays it can be sold in different forms and packaging. Some clay is further processed to suit industries with special requirements.

A cylindrical mill for disintegrating clay. On the left hand side is a combustion chamber enabling hot air to be drawn through the mill. Clay is fed into the mill from a hopper behind the cylinder and milled clay is drawn out through the pipe on the right hand side.

China clay as dried

Most clay is sold in the form which emerges from dryers or tube presses. This consists of clay lumps, which are formed by the aggregation of the ultra-fine individual particles of clay. These pellets or lumps may be loaded directly into road, rail and sea transport, or packed into large bags before loading.

Milled Clay (Also see plant illustration on previous page)

Customers in the paint, rubber and plastics industries wish to use their clay as a dry powder and for their purposes lump clay is disintegrated in a special milling machine, which also dries the clay to a moisture content of 1%. The resultant powder is packed into dust-tight paper bags.

A mill for this purpose consists of vertical rotor inside a cylinder. The rotor carries four discs with a series of small vertical blades around their edges. The discs are interspaced with larger plain discs. The rotor revolves at a speed of about 1,500 revolutions per minute and draws in a current of air which has been heated. Clay lumps are fed into the lower part of the mill. The hot air turbulence created by the rotor causes lumps of clay to dry further and collide with each other so gradually breaking down in size. The air current carries this clay up through the mill where further turbulence reduces the clay to a fine powder.

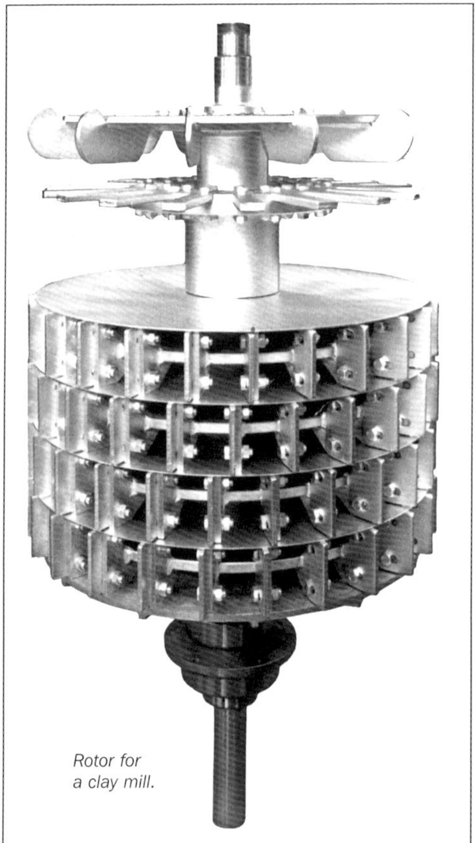

Rotor for a clay mill.

The powder is drawn through pipes, by fans, to machinery which packs the clay into strong paper bags and wraps 40 or 50 bags together with a polythene sheet. An alternative route is for the milled clay to be drawn into silos. Here it can be packed into 'intermediate bulk containers' (I.B.C.s) which are large bags each holding up to one and one quarter tonnes, or to road tankers for direct delivery to customers' silos.

Slurried Clay

Customers in the paper industry use their clay in suspension with water. This has led some customers to buy undried clay in suspension. There is some cost involved in the transport of water, but this can be offset against the handling and power costs, associated with mixing dry clay with water at the paper mill. For these customers, a thick suspension of clay and water, called slurry, is prepared and this can be pumped into road and rail tank wagons, or specially adapted ships.

Tanker wagons carrying slurry clay from Cornwall to Scotland for papermaking. This 1,200 mile round trip is the longest rail haul in the UK.

Calcined Clay for Speciality Products – Multi-hearth Kilns

If china clay is heated to temperatures above 450°c the crystalline structure of it alters and there are improvements in properties such as electrical insulation value and whiteness compared to the original. The new properties make the product of particular use in the plastics, rubber, paint and concrete industries. The heating process is known as calcination and some clay is treated to make a range of products by calcining at different temperatures.

China clay to be calcined is usually milled to a fine powder before entering the top of a multi-hearth calcining kiln shown diagrammatically overleaf.

The kiln is a large upright cylinder with a series of hearths heated by gas or oil burners. A central rotating shaft with arms pushes clay down from hearth to hearth passing the clay alternately inwards and outwards so that

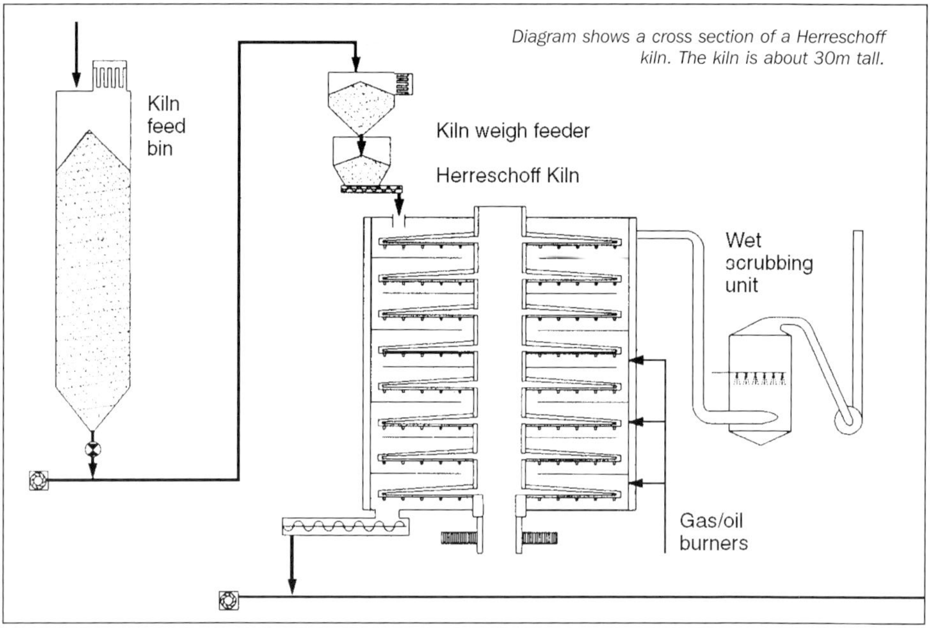

Diagram shows a cross section of a Herreschoff kiln. The kiln is about 30m tall.

An inspection door is open to show one of the arms which moves clay through the Herreschoff kiln.

after about 30 minutes of 'drench' calcining the clay emerges as a calcined product. There is some fusion of particles during the process so that the calcined clay is milled again to a fine powder for use by the customer. In this type of calciner, known as a Herreschoff Kiln, clay is calcined at temperatures from 500°c to 1100°c. One of the novel applications of clay calcined in this kiln is as an additive for concrete to prevent 'concrete cancer'.

Calcined Clay for Refractory Products - Tunnel Kilns

By heating in a different form of calciner at temperatures from 850°c to 1500°c a range of products with outstanding heat resisting properties known as 'refractories' can be prepared. For this process, long heated tunnels are used.

Clay is dried to 20% moisture and afterwards formed, by extruding machinery, into rectangular briquettes. These are placed onto flat wagons and put into a tunnel drier for a period of 32 hours at 240°c and then into a tunnel calciner for 48 hours at a maximum temperature of 1500°c. As one wagon comes out, another goes in and wagons in the tunnels move forward. The tunnel calciner has gas fired burners placed on either side. During calcination the bricks are converted to a hard, refractory product. All fired bricks are crushed and separated into different sizes. Important uses for the main product, trade named Molochite, are for making moulds in the investment casting process and to form the small spacing pieces, or 'kiln funiture', used to separate china items being fired in a potter's kiln.

Another product made in tunnel kilns is clay calcined at 550°c. This is sold for use in the manufacture of ultramarine, a blue pigment which has been made with china clay and other components since the mid-nineteenth century.

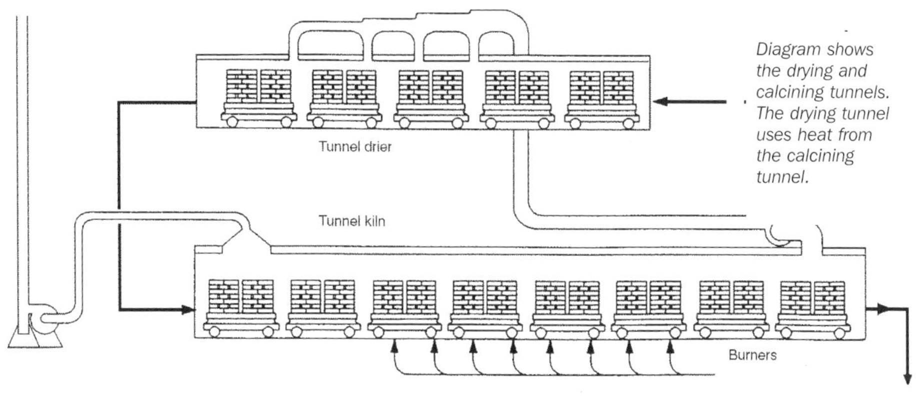

Diagram shows the drying and calcining tunnels. The drying tunnel uses heat from the calcining tunnel.

Briquettes of china clay which have first been dried and then calcined in a tunnel kiln at a maximum temperature of 1500°c. The briquettes are crushed and graded.

Flash Calcining

A novel method of calcining uses a special rapid heating process at around 850°c to heat a fine clay very quickly. This has the effect of creating tiny, sealed voids within the kaolin particles. As a result the opacity or covering power of calcined particles together with whiteness is increased. These are properties of importance for clay used in paints.

The rapid heating used in this process means that the product does not become hard as in other calcining treatments so the process is referred to as 'soft' calcining. The product is known as 'Opacilite'.

Distribution by Rail, Road and Sea

The counties of Cornwall and Devon can produce around three million tonnes of china clay per year. Well over 80% of this tonnage is sold overseas, mainly to European countries. Clay distribution includes the use of road, rail and sea transport, with stores of clay in this country and overseas, ensuring continuity of supply to customers.

In Victorian times an extensive rail network grew up in the china clay district, to serve the needs of the industry. Although many of these branch lines have since closed, all the modern dryers are rail connected. Just over half of the clay sold in the UK is moved to the customer by rail. Various special rail wagons are used for carrying bulk clay and these are fitted with protective covers to keep the clay dry and prevent loss. A regular rail service carries clay to the Potteries and another service travels regularly from Cornwall to Scotland, carrying slurry clay in tankers.

China clay is usually taken from the storage linhays by shovel loaders and loaded into lorries or rail wagons. A fleet of lorries work in Cornwall within the Par and Fowey harbour areas, transferring clay to vessels at Par or to stores at Fowey. A private road using the route and tunnel of a former branch railway line, connects the ports of Par and Fowey.

32 tonnes bulk rail wagons with bottom discharge doors used to transfer china clay to stores at Fowey.

Bulk rail wagons carrying 58 tonnes of bulk clay to continental destinations.

A small proportion of clay for export, goes by road and rail, but most is shipped from the ports of Fowey and Par in Cornwall and Plymouth in Devon. Par is a tidal port and can handle cargoes of up to 3,000 tonnes, whilst Fowey has the deepest water and can load vessels with up to 12,000

Loading from store at Fowey.

tonnes. Par and Fowey each hold stocks of clay to enable vessels to be loaded rapidly. The most modern ship loading plant at Fowey, is capable of handling up to 1,000 tonnes of clay per hour. Par also has facilities for handling slurried clay.

Above: Loading one tonne bags in a ship's hold.

Ship being loaded at Fowey also showing part of the conveyor and storage facilities.

5. THE LANDSCAPE AFTER CLAYWORKING

Summary

The visual impact of open pit workings with their associated tips is considerable. In recent times much attention has been given to improving the appearance of the landscape that is created.

Disused Pits

There are many disused pits in the area mainly formed by smaller scale workings of the past. Some of these may be incorporated into current workings but most are used as reservoirs to hold water for use by the industry. Over time nature will reclaim the edges of pit areas to create habitats for a variety of wildlife.

Ruddle Pit near St Austell. A 'Sustrans' trail for walkers, cyclists and horse riders runs nearby.

A former clay pit has been used for the well known Eden Project near St Austell. Other pits have found alternative uses such as the Nanpean Football Ground established in 1936. Some pits have been let on licence to fishing clubs who stock them for recreational fishing.

Nanpean FC in the heart of the St Austell clay area formerly Victoria clay pit.

The entrance to a trout farm and fishery.

Tipping of Overburden, Rock and Sands

Sometimes it is feasible to back fill disused pits if they no longer contain china clay of economic value and are not required to hold water reserves. To date over 35 old pits have been back filled and it is anticipated that 30% of future tipping will be contained in old pits.

Some surface tipping is required. Tip design considerations have already been mentioned (page 21). The illustration below show tipping in progress.

Tree planting is often used and aims to present a natural appearance. Softwood trees are sometimes planted as 'nurse' crop before the planting of native trees which will eventually form tree lined valleys and margins.

Dumpers tipping on the edge of a tip. A bulldozer clears the edge.

The opening of the Blackpool walking trail in 2004.

Walking Trails

Several walking trails have been established on the edge of clay working areas. These give spectacular countryside views and glimpses of clay workings. The national Sustrans organisation is also building trails for walkers, cyclists and horse riders particularly in the mid Cornwall area. Over thirty miles of trails have been completed.

Hydroseeding of Tips

For some years tips have been seeded to create a stabilising cover of vegetation. This may take place in two stages. As sand tips develop, a mulch containing grass seed and fertiliser is sprayed on to the tip. The grass controls dust which might otherwise blow off tips in dry, windy weather. Once tips have reached their pre-determined height the tip will be given a smooth profile, by a bulldozer, to remove terraces formed in tipping.

Hydroseeding unit spraying the lower part of a tip. A green dye is used to identify areas that have been seeded.

Site showing a slow natural return to heathland.

Heathland Regeneration

Before clay working much of the landscape was heathland. This was made up of heathers, gorse, and rough grasses. Farmers used these areas as a source of fuel, grazing and animal bedding. On an untreated site heathland can make a slow return after clay working but the process can be speeded up by heather seeding and a little topsoil.

The heathland habitat is now recognised as internationally endangered because of heavy losses over the past hundred years. Today completed tipping areas such as Caerloggas Downs at Singlerose have been restored to heathland. Sites treated, cover over 1,800 acres so far.

Landscaping after clay working also includes the formation of small paddocks for agricultural use. Such schemes also take advantage of topsoil removed as overburden.

The reclaimed heathland at Caerloggas is now open to the public offering panoramic views of the St Austell area.

Woodland Projects

Tree planting has been used in the past to help promote a more natural appearance to tips and their surroundings.

A major new project in the mid Cornwall area is in co-operation with English Nature. Nearly 1,800 acres of Cornish broad leaved trees will be planted with eventual public access to some of the woodlands created.

6. USES OF CHINA CLAY

To satisfy the varying requirements of customers, over sixty different grades of china clay are produced. The percentage of UK clay used by different industries is:-

Paper Coating........................21%
Paper Filling..........................49%
Ceramics/Refractory.............21%
Plastics, Rubber, Paint etc...... 9%

The Paper Industry

The largest user of china clay is the paper industry where it is used for two main purposes. Relatively coarse clay is used as a filler in the manufacture of paper, to give a smooth texture and whiteness to the sheet. It also helps the paper to take printing ink without the ink spreading, as it would on paper such as blotting, which contains no filler. Papers contain up to twenty-five per cent by weight, of a white powder such as china clay, as a filler.

Fine clays are used, up to fifty per cent by weight, in a mixture with an adhesive to coat paper. The adhesive may be latex, starch or casein. The reason for coating paper which may already be filled with china clay is to produce a smoother, brighter and glossier surface to allow for high quality colour printing. A thin film of coating is run onto the paper which is then dried. After this the paper is 'calendered' by passing it between rollers which can be arranged to give a smooth, matt or glossy finish.

The Ceramics and Refractories Industries

The ceramic industries use china clay in proportions varying from twenty to sixty per cent in their 'recipes' for whiteware, which include earthenware, porcelain, bone china, china sanitaryware, electrical porcelain and wall tiles. The refractory industries use calcined clay for its heat resisting qualities.

Other Industries; Plastics, Rubber, Paint etc.

The remaining tonnage is split between industries such as paint, rubber, plastics, chemicals, sealants, adhesives and pharmaceuticals for uses as diverse as plastic trims for car wheels, fibre glass, pills and electric cable insulation.

Conclusion

The annual value of china clay sold from the United Kingdom is over £200 million and the industry employs over 3,000 people including sub-contractors. Many other countries have their own deposits of china clay and by 2000 annual world production was around 25 million tonnes. The USA was the largest producer with about 8 million tonnes, followed by the UK with an output of 2.5 million tonnes and Brazil with 1.5 million tonnes. The Ukraine and Germany each prepare about 1 million tonnes.

China clay has been worked in Cornwall and Devon for over 250 years and reserves of china clay are expected to last well into the twenty-first century. The largest company involved, Imerys Minerals, based in France is concerned with the working of industrial minerals all over the world. These include minerals for pigments and additives, building materials, refractories and ceramics.

Looking at the China Clay Industry

The Wheal Martyn China Clay Museum at Carthew, just north of St Austell, offers a history trail around an old works, indoor displays, a nature trail and a spectacular view of a modern clay pit. More displays together with a new café and shop have recently been provided by a Heritage Lottery grant.

For details telephone:
01726 850362
See website at:
www.wheal-martyn.com

Plunger pumps used for china clay working in the nineteenth century.